The Clear-Out

DEBORAH ELLIS

The Clear-Out

Grass Roots Press

First published in 2013 by Grass Roots Press

Grass Roots Press gratefully acknowledges the financial support for its publishing programs provided by the following agencies: the Government of Canada through the Canada Book Fund and the Government of Alberta through the Alberta Foundation for the Arts.

Grass Roots Press would also like to thank ABC Life Literacy Canada for their support. Good Reads® is used under licence from ABC Life Literacy Canada.

Library and Archives Canada Cataloguing in Publication

Ellis, Deborah, 1960–, author
    The clear-out / Deborah Ellis.

(Good reads)
ISBN 978–1–77153–003–3 (pbk.)

    1. Readers for new literates. I. Title. II. Series: Good reads series (Edmonton, Alta.

PS8559.L5494C54 2013   428.6'2   C2013–902654–1

To my father

CHAPTER ONE

Duncan came home from playing golf to find that his wife had lost her mind.

He came into the house through the back door. He took his shoes off and dropped them on the mat. His wife, Tess, tidied up all the shoes ten times a day.

As Duncan entered the kitchen, he looked at the chalkboard on the wall for messages. One of his golf buddies had called to pull out of their game the next day. Duncan thought about making some phone calls to find another player. First, though, he checked the kitchen clock. It was almost time for *Wide World of Golf* to start on TV.

"How did I live for all those years without the Golf Channel?" he often said. He thought it again now as he reached into the fridge for a can of beer.

With his foot, he pushed the cat, Mr. Snuffles, out of his way.

Duncan went into the living room and right to the sofa. He could sit, pick up the remote, and take a swig of beer, all in one smooth move. He put his feet up on the coffee table, clicked the TV on, and turned the volume up. Another perfect day.

And then he saw the dining room.

Or what used to be the dining room.

The dining room had doorways into both the kitchen and the living room. When he sat on the sofa, Duncan could usually see the dining room table. He could also see the big china cabinet. In it, Tess kept their good china and their wedding gifts from nearly forty years ago. She kept all the little glass animals he had given her over the years in the china cabinet, too.

But today, Duncan couldn't see any of it.

Today, he was looking at a dark wall that blocked the doorway.

"Tess!" he called out. He had to shout to make himself heard over the sound of the TV.

His wife didn't answer.

"Tess!" He turned the TV down. He knew his wife was in the house. Where else would she be? But she didn't answer.

Duncan swore, put his beer down on a coaster on the table, and got up off the sofa.

"Tess!"

To get into the dining room, he had to go back through the kitchen. He couldn't believe what he saw.

The dining room table was gone. The china cabinet doors were open. There was nothing inside the cupboard. No china. No wedding gifts, still wrapped in plastic. No little glass animals.

Duncan was gripped with a sudden fear: they had been robbed. Thugs had burst in and stolen almost everything from their dining room. But, in that case, what had they done with his wife? "Tess! Tess!"

His voice took on a new panic. Where was his wife?

"There's no need to shout."

He spun around to see Tess coming up the basement stairs into the kitchen. She carried a large cardboard box.

"Where were you? I was calling."

"As you can see, I was in the basement."

"You didn't answer me."

"I am answering you now."

He didn't like her tone. It was calm. She was not the least bit upset that he was upset.

"What have you done to the dining room? Give me that." He put his hands out to take the cardboard box from her. "You shouldn't be carrying things up the stairs. You could have fallen, and then what would you have done?"

"Gotten back up, I expect."

Tess did not give the box to Duncan. She just went past him into the dining room.

"You've made an awful mess," Duncan said. "I hope you don't expect me to put everything back the way it was!"

Tess did not answer him. She set the box down and stretched her back.

She smiled.

But she was smiling at the mess. Not at him.

"I'm making a library," she finally said.

"A library? Don't be foolish. There's a library downtown."

"I want my own."

"Well, I want my dining room back."

All she said to that was, "You're missing *Wide World of Golf.*"

He was, too, and that did not improve his mood.

"The table is downstairs," she said. "The china and everything else is packed away safely, and it's all downstairs, too."

"You couldn't take that big table downstairs."

"It came apart. I took the legs off."

"You took the legs off?"

"With a screwdriver."

Duncan open and closed his mouth like a fish. "You better not have used my tools! They're not toys, you know!"

"And I am not Bobby, so don't talk to me as if I was seven years old."

Bobby, their son, now fully grown, had finally left their house when he was twenty-eight. He had been living in their basement. When he left, Duncan turned the basement into his work-out space.

"Is that what this is?" Duncan asked. "The nest is empty, so you don't know what to do with yourself?"

"Oh, I know what to do with myself," Tess replied. "Filling my days will not be a problem for me."

She walked by him and went down the basement stairs. Duncan heard her pick up another box and climb back up. She put the box with the others, then faced him.

"It's simple," she said. "Bobby has, at long last, started his life. You have golf and all your sports things. My parents have passed away. I have retired from my job, and I get money from my pension. I have a decision to make. What do I want to do with the rest of my life? And this is it. I want to read. And I want a room to read in."

"A whole room? That's just foolish. You don't need a whole room to read in. Read in a chair. There's the entire living room out there."

"And you keep the television on. In here, I can still hear it, but at least I won't have to see it. It would be nice, as a favour to me, if you would move the TV into your sports room."

"Move the TV? This is my house. I like the TV where it is." The sports room was Bobby's childhood bedroom. Duncan now used it for his collection of sports things—baseball bobble-head dolls, hockey cards, golf trophies. A man had to have a place to display his things.

Tess just shrugged. She reached behind a pile of books and brought out a box of ear plugs.

"I thought you would say that," she said.

"What about the dining room?" Duncan asked. "What about family dinners? What about Christmas?"

"Christmas is just one day. We can eat in the kitchen. All around the world, people manage to get their families together without a formal dining room."

"I don't know what's come over you," Duncan said.

"That's all right," said Tess. "You're missing your show."

Duncan stood in the doorway and watched his wife. She smiled and hummed as she put the books on the shelves of the cabinet. Tess had wanted to put the books out years ago. But Duncan insisted that there wasn't room, and books made a house look too cluttered. Now they were being put into the cabinet that used to hold their wedding gifts.

Even worse, Tess had lined up tall bookshelves across the doorway that had opened to the living room. She had closed the space off. He was going

13

to ask where she had gotten the shelves. Then he remembered seeing them, boxed up, behind the furnace. He had thought they belonged to their son.

Duncan didn't know that Tess knew how to put up shelves.

"It's good to know that you could put our wedding gifts in the basement without even thinking about it," he said. "It's good to know how you really feel about our marriage."

"Those gifts are just things," Tess said. She did not look up from her books.

CHAPTER TWO

Tess got more books and more bookshelves.

She bought a La-Z-Boy chair and put a little table and a good reading lamp beside it. She made the room her own.

The cat, Mr. Snuffles, sat by her feet, purring as she read.

Duncan fought back.

He did not like looking at the wall made of bookshelves. He did not like having a wife who did not answer when he called.

He tried to move the television into Tess's library.

Tess put her foot down.

"I want one room in this house that is mine," she said. "I've cleaned this house and earned money to help pay for it. I deserve a space in it that is mine. If you want *this* space, then I will take over your sports room. If you won't let me have that, then I will take over your work-out room. And if you won't let me have *that*, then I will take my pension and my savings and leave. I'll move to my own apartment with my books."

"One of these days," Duncan said, "I'll get rid of all these books and put my dining room back."

"You can do that," Tess said, "but you had better be ready for what happens next."

He never tried it.

Tess did allow Duncan to move another chair into the room. He would sit in there with her sometimes.

But he was not used to sitting without a TV in front of him, and he had never liked reading.

When he tried to talk to her, she put her book down and let him talk. But he knew she was just waiting for him to be done so she could go back to her reading.

Duncan hated the books. He hated them for what they were doing to his wife.

Before she retired, Tess worked as a secretary in a law office. Her clothes were always pressed and her hair was always done.

16

bother عذاب دینا

Once she got her library, all that changed. She got her hair cut very short. When Duncan asked her why, she told him, "I don't want to be bothered with my hair."

He told her he didn't like it short. Tess said he would get used to it.

She also stopped wearing makeup.

"How I look is not important to me anymore," she said.

Tess gave away all her small purses and started carrying a shoulder bag big enough to hold a book. She always had a book with her. She would read her book whenever she felt like it, no matter what else was going on around her.

Tess even took one of her books to the annual clubhouse dinner at the golf course. Duncan had gone to the bar for a while to chat with his golf buddies. When he came back to the table, she was not talking with the other wives. She was reading her book!

He took the book away from her. In front of everyone. She called a taxi and went home without him.

Tess and Duncan went on this way. Duncan got used to it. But he never liked it.

Then, one day, Cancer walked into the house.

No matter what they did, they could not get it to leave.

CHAPTER THREE

After her second operation for cancer, Tess was too weak to go upstairs. Her library became her sick room.

The La-Z-Boy went into the living room. In its place was their son's old single bed. The first-floor bathroom was close by, and so was the kitchen.

The books now stood in piles on the floor, and the shelves held the things Tess needed to get through the day. Medicines and clean sheets and nightgowns filled several shelves. On one shelf were the adult diapers for when Tess was too weak to walk to the toilet.

Home care nurses and other help came and went. Duncan hated having strangers in his house. He would turn on the Golf Channel while they looked after Tess. Staring at the TV, he tried not to think about what was happening on the other side of the wall.

The helpers visited during the day. At night, Duncan slept on the sofa. That way, he could hear Tess if she needed him in the middle of the night.

Tess's hair fell out with the cancer treatment. Duncan bought her hats to keep her head warm. Hats with flowers, hats with pompoms, hats in bright colours. He looked for hats everywhere he went. If he found the right hat, it would fix everything. That's what his heart told him, anyway.

When Tess felt well enough, she read in bed.

One night, Duncan stood in the kitchen door and watched her. When her eyes started to close from the effect of the drugs, she shook herself awake and kept reading.

Are you afraid? he wanted to ask her. Did you have a good life? Do you regret anything? Did I make you happy?

He wanted to ask her all of those questions. But he couldn't ask any of them. He was too far out of the habit of talking with his wife.

"Enough reading for tonight," he said instead, and he started to take the book from her.

"But I'm almost finished!"

"Finish it later," Duncan said. "You need to rest."

Taking the book away from Tess was easy. She had no more strength in her hands. She could not hold on to the book. It slid through her pale, thin fingers.

"I want to know how the story ends," Tess said.

"There is plenty of time for that." Duncan put the book on one of the piles in the corner of the room.

"I want my book back," Tess said from her bed.

"Forget the book," Duncan snapped. "Who cares about a book? Talk to me! I am your husband!"

"I want to know what happens!"

"Talk to me!" Duncan took hold of her hand. "Be with me!"

"I want to know …"

Tess started to cough, a thin, kitten-like cough.

"Do you need some water?" Duncan asked.

He picked up the jug he kept on the shelf of the china cupboard. It was empty. "I'll get you some water."

He took the jug into the kitchen. He let the water run until it was as cold as it would get. He kicked himself for not keeping water in the fridge.

He filled the jug, brought it back into the sick room, and poured his wife a glass.

He put his hand under Tess's head to raise her up so she could take a drink.

That was when he knew that she was gone.

CHAPTER FOUR

Nothing is quite as empty as a house after a funeral.

Bobby took apart the bed in the sick room and got rid of the stuff of death. After a few days, Duncan had to insist that his son leave. It had taken Bobby months to find that job in the city. Duncan didn't want the boy to risk losing it by taking too many days off.

Besides, there was nothing for Bobby to do. The funeral was over, and the paperwork was done. The good ladies of the church had delivered their pies and one-dish suppers. The fellows from the golf club had slapped Duncan's back in sympathy and slipped him some bottles of gin. There was nothing left to do now.

Duncan took a beer out of the fridge and sat on the sofa. He put his feet on the coffee table and picked up the remote control. *Wide World of Golf* was on. He turned up the volume.

"Tess!" he called out.

Then he started crying.

Duncan cried for a long time. He cried until his head ached and his shirt front was wet. Then he looked up from his tears to the wall made by the backs of the bookshelves.

He hated those shelves! He hated those books! He hated what they had done to his wife. They had changed her from a smiling, busy little woman into some strange person. A thing that frowned and thought and tried to understand things that no one had any business trying to understand.

Well, she was gone now, and he didn't have to put up with the library any longer. And he wouldn't. Not one more minute!

Duncan reached under the kitchen sink, grabbed the box of garbage bags, marched into the dining room. He started filling the bags with books. He grabbed them all and threw them in the bags, stuffing the bags as full as he could without breaking them.

"Those books are just good for garbage," he said. He started to take the bags out to the curb but stopped by his car instead. The books weren't any good to him, but they might be good for someone, and he hated throwing things away.

Duncan took his golf clubs out of the car's trunk to make more room. He filled the trunk, then the back seat, and even the front seat. But he got all the bags in.

He had to back out of his driveway carefully. Five or six skateboarders were spinning around the turning circle in front of his house, Duncan honked his horn to get them to move.

He drove downtown, to the Good Shepherd Thrift Store.

"You take books?"

A man sat behind the counter wearing a badge with "Volunteer" written on it. He turned his head to face the wall of books that ran along the side of the shop.

"What kind of books?" he asked.

"What do you mean, what kind?" Duncan asked. "I don't know what kind. Books."

"Well, we do take them," the volunteer said. "Are they good books?"

"They're books."

Duncan spoke the word as if it was a curse.

25

"I mean, are they clean? We don't need bookworms or bugs."

"There are no bugs in my house," Duncan snarled. "If you don't want the books, I'll take them to the dump."

"Let's take a look at them," the volunteer said. "Do you have them with you?"

"They're in the car. It's parked out front." Duncan waited for the volunteer to get up and help him.

For a moment, the volunteer didn't move, but then he picked up the hint. "Let's go get them," he said, as if the job was something bright and shiny and fun to do. As he moved out from behind the counter, Duncan saw the wheelchair.

"Sorry, I didn't see—"

"Load me up," the volunteer said. "I can't feel anything anyway. Might as well make myself useful. I'm Kevin."

Kevin held out his hand. Duncan shook it and shared his own name. "What happened to your legs?" he asked. He wouldn't usually ask such a nosy question, but his wife had just died. That meant he could do what he liked.

"Got beat up," Kevin said.

"What?"

"Coming out of the hardware store. Can you believe it? I got lucky," Kevin said. "Only paralyzed below the waist. My husband didn't make it."

"Your husband."

Once Duncan would have been shocked or disgusted. But cancer changes everything. Now he just wanted to know one thing.

"How do you manage?" he asked. "My wife just died."

The two men looked at each other.

Kevin shook his head. "Let's get those books."

They made several trips. The black garbage bags made quite a pile on the floor.

"She was always reading. Drove me crazy."

"Dan was always volunteering," Kevin said. "*That* drove *me* crazy. And look at me now."

Duncan didn't want to look. He didn't want to think. He didn't want to feel. He didn't want to do anything but put his dining room back together and get drunk.

So that's what he did. He went home and carried the parts of the dining room table up from the basement. How had his tiny little wife got them down the stairs in the first place? He screwed the legs back on. Next, he put the china and Tess's little glass animals back in the china cabinet. Then he opened one of the bottles of gin he got from his golf buddies. He stayed drunk for a week.

CHAPTER FIVE

Months went by.

Life went on.

That was the worst part about death, Duncan thought one morning as he was pulling on his socks. He had put on socks when Tess was alive, and he was still putting on socks now that she was dead.

For a very short time, her death was important. People cried. They talked about her. They gave him things to try to cheer him up. But time passed. Life went on. It went on without Tess.

And, every morning, Duncan put on a clean pair of socks. Just as if nothing had happened.

He was managing okay. That's what he told people when they asked: "I'm managing okay."

He had a freezer full of frozen dinners. He often bought a roasted chicken. He learned how to work the washing machine and dryer. He could run the vacuum cleaner, and he knew how to use the dust cloth. When he ran out of something, he wrote it on the chalkboard so he could remember to buy more.

As always, he put his dirty coffee cup in the sink. But it was not washed and back in the cupboard the next time he reached for it. That was the hardest thing to get used to.

When the pile of shoes by the door got messy, it stayed messy. No unseen hand straightened it up for him.

Wherever he dropped stuff, that's where it stayed. If it got picked up, he had to do it.

At first, Duncan let the mess grow. Tess was supposed to clean the house, damn it. If she didn't do her job, he sure wasn't going to do it for her! He had his own things to do—mowing the lawn, hosing down the driveway. Things like that.

His feelings changed the day their minister, Reverend Jones, dropped in. Duncan saw his mess through the other man's eyes. Ashamed about what he had done to his wife's clean house, he thought about hiring a cleaner. But he could not stand the thought of another stranger in his home. Way too many strangers had come in and out when his wife was sick. Visiting nurses, home-care workers, busybody neighbours.

The worst were the members of his wife's book club. They would sit with her and hold her hand and chatter quietly, as though they had some big secret. They stole time from him. He could barely stand to look at them at the funeral.

So he had to learn to pick up after himself.

"I hope you're happy, Tess," Duncan muttered to her as he dried and put away his dishes. "You finally got me to do housework."

Other things changed, too.

He could no longer watch the Golf Channel. He tried after the funeral, but he couldn't do it. It just wasn't fun anymore. He realized that it was fun when Tess was alive because it proved he was running his own show. Tess didn't like golf, but he was his own man. He could watch and play golf whenever he wanted to. Now that sort of thinking held no meaning.

But there were other channels. Duncan watched a lot of reality TV and the channel that showed old movies. Between television and little errands around town, he could fill up a day. He did not look back,

DEBORAH ELLIS

and he did not look into the future. This moment, the one he was in, was all he could manage.

Three months after Tess died, strange things started happening.

Duncan didn't notice them at first.

And when he did, he put them down to old age. He got into the habit of tidying the house every night after the eleven o'clock news. He would walk through the rooms, picking up any stray papers, putting away any stray dishes. He put the newspaper in the blue box and tidied the shoes on the mat by the kitchen door. Alone now, Duncan feared falling if he got up in the middle of the night. He liked to know the stairs and the floor were clear of anything he could trip over. And, he noticed, waking up to a tidy house was nicer than starting the day in a mess.

One morning, as Duncan made his coffee, he noticed that the shoes were all messed up.

"Must have forgotten to do that last night," he said to the cat. He was sure he had lined up the shoes. He always did. But each day was so much like the last. He could have forgotten.

He made sure he tidied the shoes that night.

The next morning, they were messed up again.

"Maybe I'm sleepwalking," he said.

When the same thing happened again the next night, he decided he was just going crazy.

"If that's as crazy as I get, I can live with it," he said.

One morning when he got up, all the dining room chairs had been upset.

He blamed the cat.

"Do it again and I'll drop you at the Humane Society," he said to Mr. Snuffles. Mr. Snuffles just yawned and turned his back. The chairs kept getting knocked over in the night.

The cat acted strangely, too.

Mr. Snuffles started to sit for hours on the carpet by Tess's La-Z-Boy, purring. Just like he did when Tess used to sit in that chair and read. At night, he ran around the house, jumping and waving his paws in the air. Tess used to knit little mice and stuff them with catnip. She tied them to long strings, and she'd play mousie with him all over the house. Now the cat seemed to be playing with a mousie that only he could see.

The cat's game was funny to watch. But it was less funny when Mr. Snuffles bounded across Duncan's bed in the middle of the night.

Duncan found closet doors open that he knew he had closed. The TV would turn itself off in the middle of a show. The TV remote would be lost for days, then suddenly show up in the fridge next to the prune juice.

One Sunday, Duncan hung back after church to be the last to shake the minister's hand. He needed advice.

"Grief takes many forms," Reverend Jones said. "You have had a terrible loss. Give yourself time to get used to it. Get out into the community. Be with people. Many people hold you in high regard. Give them the gift of letting them support you."

Duncan knew that was a standard speech because not many people held him in high regard. Why would they? He had never done anything for them. He had never really done anything for anybody. He played in charity golf games, but he did it for the golf, not for the charity.

He learned to live with the strange events. Every morning he re-tidied the shoes by the door and turned the dining room chairs right side up.

At night, he closed his bedroom door so the cat couldn't play with <u>invisible</u> mousies on top of him.

He managed everything else in his life, the cooking, the cleaning, the <u>loneliness.</u> He could manage these <u>strange events</u>, too.

And then one day Duncan walked into the kitchen and stopped managing.

There <u>were</u> words on the chalkboard.

Words he knew he had not <u>put</u> there.

He stood in icy <u>shock</u> and read them.

What happens?

The words were written in his wife's handwriting.

CHAPTER SIX

"So I'm not crazy."

"You are sad," the Reverend Jones said. "Grief takes time. People get on with their days and take care of business, and they think their grief is all over. But it isn't. It takes time."

Duncan looked down at his hands. He was sitting across from the minister in his office at the church.

"Have you ever . . . lost someone?" he asked.

"We have all had losses in our lives," the minister replied. "I have talked with many in our church who have lost someone in their family. Grief is a powerful feeling. People often think they see their loved one in a shopping mall or on the street. Or they see the much loved face in the window of a moving bus. The person always seems just out of reach."

"Has anyone at our church seen his dead wife's handwriting on the wall?"

The minister smiled. "No. That's a new one. But let's look at what was written. 'What happens?' Is that the sort of message likely to come from the other side? You should look into this very carefully. I think you'll find that you wrote those words yourself. Maybe you did it in your sleep. Maybe you're wondering what happens next with your life."

"So what should I do?"

"Pray. Rest. Go out for walks. Eat well. Take up something new. Give your mind something different to focus on. And give yourself time."

As he drove away from the church, Duncan thought maybe he needed another seven-day drunk.

The skateboarders were at it again when he drove into his street. They blasted their loud, awful music as they skated around. Instead of yelling at them, Duncan just sat and watched them, zooming round and round in front of his driveway.

"Maybe skateboarding is the new thing I should take up," he said to himself.

Then he leaned on the car horn until the skateboarders got the message. They took off, wind blowing their hair, not a care in the world.

37

"Rotten kids," Duncan muttered. He drove into his garage and went into his house.

He rubbed out the words on the chalkboard and turned on the TV.

When he went back into the kitchen to make himself a sandwich, the words were back.

The same words.

The same handwriting.

What happens?

"Enough with this nonsense!" Duncan shouted. He grabbed the chalkboard and tore it from the wall. He stomped out of the kitchen and through the back door. He dumped the chalkboard into the trash can and clamped the lid on the can. Then he took the can out to the curb.

That night, he slept with his bedroom door open. The cat left him alone. The closet doors stayed shut. At dawn, he heard the garbage truck coming around his circle. His trash can banged against the truck, and the truck took away the chalkboard.

Duncan slept in until eight. He stretched in his bed, fully rested, then got up and padded to the kitchen in his bare feet and pajamas. Why not have coffee *before* getting dressed? He wouldn't make a habit of it, but why not shake his life up a bit? After all, he was retired. He had nowhere to go and no one to ask him why he was still in his pajamas. He filled the kettle, then turned to get the jar of instant coffee out of the cupboard.

The chalkboard was back on the wall.
In the same spot.
With the same words.
In the same handwriting.

What happens?

And that's when Duncan got really scared.

CHAPTER SEVEN

Duncan was almost afraid to get close to the chalkboard, but he had to get it out of the house.

With a pounding heart and a dry mouth, he took the chalkboard down from the wall—again. Scooping up his keys, he put the chalkboard in the passenger seat of his car. He got in behind the wheel and started driving.

The Good Shepherd Thrift Store was not open yet. Duncan didn't care. He sat in his car in his pajamas, his feet still bare, staring at the chalkboard.

As soon as he spotted Kevin coming around the corner in his wheelchair, Duncan jumped out of the car. He had the chalkboard in his hand.

"Get rid of this," he ordered.

Kevin looked him up and down.

"What happened to you?" he asked.

"I need you to get rid of this for me."

"It says, 'What happens?'" Kevin said.

"I know what it says. I need you to get rid of it."

Kevin took the shop keys out of his shirt pocket. "Let's go inside. I think we could both use some coffee." He locked the door behind them so they would not be bothered by customers.

Kevin had the same brand of instant coffee in the back of the shop that Duncan had at home. The two men waited for the water to boil. Duncan sat down on a box. Kevin held out his hand for the chalkboard.

"By 'get rid of it,' I take it that you don't want me to just sell it in the shop."

"I need it gone."

Kevin handed Duncan a cup of coffee. "What's going on?"

Duncan leaned up against a stack of boxes. "When you lost your ... husband ... did you ... did anything strange happen?"

"Strange? What do you mean by strange?"

"Do I have to spell it out?"

"Yes! You have to spell it out. I can't guess what's in your head. You are standing here in your

41

PJs and bare feet. I don't think you are crazy, but I don't know what you're trying to tell me. Why do you need me to get rid of this chalkboard?"

"Because it's haunted!" Duncan yelled. "It's haunted by my dead wife! She's in the whole house, opening doors, playing with the cat, messing up the shoes. I can't get rid of my whole house. But I can at least get rid of this chalkboard and this horrible message."

Kevin raised his hand and wiped the words off the board.

"Oh, very good," Duncan said. "I never would have thought of that. I'm cold," he suddenly realized.

"There are clean clothes on that rack over there," Kevin said. "Help yourself."

Duncan wrapped himself in a grey robe and sat down on his box again.

"My minister says it takes time, that all I'm experiencing is part of grief. I can accept that. That makes sense. But this does not make sense. I wipe out the message and it appears again. I throw away the board and it's back again in the morning. Maybe I *am* just sleepwalking. I don't have any friends I can ask. I'm nearly seventy years old, and I have no friends I can have a serious conversation with. You are the only one who can give me real answers. Did this happen to you when your husband died?"

Kevin took a sip of coffee. Then he put the cup down and leaned forward with his elbows on his knees.

"Not right away," he said. "I was in the hospital for a while. Then I had to have help at home while I learned how to live in a wheelchair. But at last all the home-care workers and friends and family went back to their own lives. I was alone. That's when the strange things started."

Kevin rubbed his hands together.

"I thought I was over Dan's death," he said. "I was managing okay. Life was different, but I was doing all right. And then things started happening. I'd smell Dan's aftershave. The knives, forks, and spoons would get messed up in the cutlery drawer. I like everything in its place. Dan could never see the point in that. When I'd go to bed, all the cutlery would be in its proper place. But in the morning, the knives, forks, and spoons would be all mixed together."

"You think he was there?"

"He was there for sure. You know what it's like when you come into your house and it's empty? Or when you come in, and it's quiet, but you can tell someone is there? Dan was there."

They drank their coffee in silence for a moment.

"What does 'What happens?' mean?" Kevin asked.

"I don't know. Maybe it doesn't mean anything. Did you get any messages from Dan?"

"The number 75," Kevin said. "It kept appearing. Written in the dust on the telephone table. On the mirror when I got out of the shower. All kinds of places."

"What did it mean?"

"Turns out, Dan had life insurance. Seven hundred and fifty thousand dollars' worth. He just hadn't got around to telling me while he was alive."

"Seven hundred and fifty thousand. Wow. That's life-changing money."

"And I've changed my life."

"How did you figure it out?" Duncan asked.

"I took a leap of faith."

Duncan could get no more information out of him. They heard someone banging on the shop door.

"Leave me your phone number, Duncan," Kevin said. "I'll set something up."

"What?"

"Leap of faith, my friend. We'll talk tomorrow."

The parking lot was busy with shoppers and cars when Duncan left the thrift store. As he walked to his car, he kept his eyes straight ahead. If people were staring at him in his pajamas, he didn't want to know.

CHAPTER EIGHT

Two days after Duncan gave Kevin the chalkboard, Kevin asked Duncan to come to the thrift shop. There, in the shop's storage room, stood the leader of the skateboard boys.

The kid wiped his nose on his shirt sleeve. He tossed his long hair off his face, and it flopped right back down into his eyes again.

"You have got to be kidding," Duncan said.

"That was my reaction, too," Kevin said. "Wait until you hear him."

"I've heard him," Duncan said. "I've heard his loud music and his rude tone. Teenagers today don't care about anybody but themselves. I'm getting out of here."

"She's trying to ask you something, bro," the skateboarder said. "And she's getting a little annoyed with you."

"Don't you speak of her!" Duncan spun on the boy, pointing his finger right under the boy's nose. "She was worth more than you and your lazy friends put together will ever be worth."

"Then maybe you should have treated her better when she was alive, bro."

"I'm not your bro. And I'm leaving."

"Peace out, then," the kid said.

Duncan stomped out of the thrift store. His car tires squealed as he sped out of the parking lot. "I don't have to put up with this," he muttered. "I can sell the house. Why not? It's mine. I'll sell it, take the money, and go someplace warm and play golf all year. I'm single now. Time to start acting single!"

He'd go visit a real estate agent that very morning. The kid on the skateboard zoomed by him, darting in and out of traffic. He looked as if he was flying.

"I hope you get run over!" Duncan yelled. "I hope you get smashed up! Why should *you* get to live, when better people than you have to die?"

Duncan didn't know why he had waited so long to leave town. Really, the time had come.

Was his passport up to date? He'd need to make a list of things to do. How should he sell his furniture? Maybe the real estate agent would know someone who could come in and deal with it all.

Duncan thought for a moment about asking his son for help, but he decided against it. Bobby would have strong feelings about selling the family home. And Duncan didn't want to know about them.

He didn't want to know, and he didn't want to care. All he wanted was to play golf. Play golf, lie on some beach, and drink himself silly for the rest of his life.

"It's *my* life," he muttered. "I can finally do with it what *I* want to do."

To drown out his thoughts, Duncan turned on the car radio. He tried to find a station that would come in clearly, but all he got was static. "Must be a storm somewhere," he said.

Finally, he got an oldies station. He sat back to enjoy songs that were new when he was young.

And then the music stopped.

And Duncan heard the words.

They were almost whispered, but he heard them loud and clear.

What happens?

And Duncan drove straight into a telephone pole.

As he sat there, his right fender crunched up, strangers rushed over to see if he was all right. Police sirens came closer and closer. Duncan wished he had just stayed in bed.

"Come back, Tess," he said. "I want to go home."

CHAPTER NINE

Duncan had never been to the skateboard park. The town had built the park last year, and Duncan was angry that it had been paid for with tax money. He had written a letter to the editor of the local newspaper. "Why do kids need to skateboard?" he had written. "Walking is free. If their parents want them to have a skateboard park, then let their parents pay for it."

And now, there he was, at the very same park.

He sat on a bench, and Kevin sat in his chair. They drank Tim Hortons coffee and watched kids on skateboards roll up and over cement cliffs.

"What in the world would make someone want to do that?" Duncan asked.

"You must have done some crazy things in your life," Kevin said. "Everyone has. Or if you didn't do crazy things, you wanted to."

"I worked," Duncan said. "I paid my bills. I played a lot of golf."

"Not much to write on your gravestone, is it?"

"Will the writing on yours be any better?"

"I'm a proud gay man. That in itself is a sign of success."

Duncan couldn't think of anything to say to that, so he said nothing.

"There he is," Kevin said, spotting the kid they were looking for. "Hey, Fly King! Over here!"

"Fly King?" Duncan asked.

"That's his skate name."

"Do I have to call him that?"

"He's doing you a favour," Kevin reminded him. "Would it kill you to be nice?"

Fly King took his time coming over. He skated up and down the valleys, going around and doing jumps off the ramps. Duncan had to admit that the kid was good. Not that he was any judge of skateboarders.

Fly King skated right up to them, stopped, and picked up his board in one smooth motion. He did not seem surprised to see them.

"She wants to know what happens," Fly King said.

"She wants to know what happens to what? To me? Is she worried about me?"

The kid laughed.

"The book, man," the kid said. "She wants to know what happens in the book."

"What book?"

"The book she was reading when she kicked it."

Duncan came close to hitting the kid.

"What book?"

"How should I know?" Fly King replied. "Don't you know? You were there, man."

"Ask her," Duncan demanded.

"Doesn't work that way." Fly King put his skateboard back on the ground. "I don't talk to them. They talk to me. And only when they feel like it. They're dead. They do what they want."

"What am I supposed to do now?" Duncan asked. He didn't feel any closer to knowing what was going on.

"Read the book, bro. Tell her what happens."

In the next moment, the kid was gone, dropping down into a cement valley.

"There were so many books," Duncan said. "I don't know what she was reading at the end."

"How can you not know that?" Kevin said. "Didn't you ask her?"

"She was always reading," Duncan said. "I asked her all the time, 'What are you reading?'"

The full question he had asked was, *What are you reading that for?*

As if he could hear Duncan's thoughts, Kevin asked, "Did you ever listen to her answer?"

Duncan didn't reply. Of course he hadn't listened to her answer. In the beginning, she would tell him what she was reading, thinking he might be truly interested. But his eyes would gloss over and his ears would shut. He had not asked her so that he could learn something. He had asked her only to make her talk to him.

Duncan looked at the books on the thrift shop shelves. "All these books," he said. "I'm going to have to go through all these books. And what about the ones you sold already? What if it's one of them? Finding the one she didn't finish is impossible."

"Now, hang on a minute," Kevin said. "Don't give up. Let's think. What do you remember about that day?"

"I remember Tess dying. What do you think I remember?"

"You must remember something about the book. Think. Did it have a hard cover or was it a paperback? Did the cover have a picture on it? Was it a big thick book or a little skinny book?"

Duncan thought back to that terrible day. He could see his wife, his Tess, tiny on the bed. Her arm reached out to hold on to the book he was taking away. It was not a good picture.

"She was weak," he said. "The book would not have been heavy."

"So, small and skinny. Good. We can pass by a lot of these, then."

Duncan picked up some of the paperback books. He held them in his hand to try to remember.

"These don't feel right," he said. "Something about the weight or the shape. And the cover was shiny. Smooth."

The book had slid right out of her fingers. Even so, he had felt her slight grip, trying to hold on to it.

"Good," Kevin said. "We are probably looking for a small, skinny book with a shiny paper cover on it." He started going through the shelves, pulling books out that might look like that.

Duncan kept thinking. He started to get angry.

"All I did for her," he said. "She had a good life. She never had anything to complain about. I didn't drink. I didn't smoke. I didn't run around with other women. I provided a good home for her and our son. Such a good home that Bobby didn't want to leave it. And she wanted to read more than she wanted to talk with me."

He threw the books in his hand down on the floor.

"Let her haunt me," he said. "At least now she has to talk to me."

And he stomped out of the store.

CHAPTER TEN

Duncan did not believe in looking inside himself.

He saw no point in sitting around, thinking about how things could have been. There was what happened, and there was today, and there was tomorrow. The only way to get on in life was to deal with the world that was right in front of you. Anything else was ... well, nothing good would come of living in the past.

When he got home from the shop, there was a message on the answering machine from his son. Bobby was coming for a visit.

Duncan looked around. The house could use tidying up. He had let things slip a bit. He didn't want Bobby to think he couldn't manage.

"To heck with it," he said. "Let the kid do the cleaning. I've spent plenty of time picking up after him."

Besides, he needed to sell the place. Duncan called a real estate agent. The agent could come over right away.

"This is a very nice property, Mr. Brown," the agent said. He walked from room to room with a pen clipped to a clipboard and a phone clipped to his ear. "What are you hoping to get for it?"

"I bought the house twenty years ago," he said. "I'm expecting to get a lot more than I paid for it."

"You have taken care of it very well," the agent said. "But there are a few things you could do to update it. A bit of paint here. Maybe replace the counter top in the kitchen. Now, about this dining room. No one uses dining rooms anymore. Families do not have the time to eat together. People will not know what to do with this space. Have you thought of giving it a different use—turning it into something else?"

The agent turned and looked Duncan right in the eye. Suddenly, the man seemed to be wearing a different face. "Have you thought about maybe turning it into ... a library?" he asked.

Something about the way the agent spoke, something about his voice or his rude smile scared Duncan. Or something about the words themselves. A chill ran from the tips of Duncan's toes to the brush-cut hairs on the top of his head.

"Get out!" he yelled. "Go! Get out, right now!"

Anger replaced the strange look on the real estate agent's face. "You can't treat me like that!" he said. "I'm going to report you to the real estate board. No one will help you. You'll be stuck with this house forever!"

"Get out!" Duncan kept screaming.

The agent ran out to his car and backed down the driveway. He almost hit one of the skateboard boys who were circling around yet again.

"What happens?" the skateboard boys yelled at Duncan.

Duncan slammed the door on all of them.

"I'll sell the house myself," he said. All he needed was a sign. He had an old election sign in his basement. Tess had put this sign on the lawn because she wanted people to vote for some foolish young man. Duncan had pulled the stupid sign out of the lawn and hidden it.

He would paint over that old election sign and have it on the lawn when his son arrived. That would give Bobby the message, loud and clear. He, Duncan, was about to lead his own life for once.

The basement stairs led directly into the rec room. Duncan had put up the wood panelling himself. For way too long, the room had been his son's home. Now it held a treadmill and some weights and other gym equipment. Duncan hadn't used any of it since Tess died.

He crossed the rec room and opened the door into the workshop.

There was paint everywhere.

All over the back room of the basement, on the floor, on the walls. Even on the water heater, on the washer and dryer.

All colours of leftover paint. Paint collected over years of painting bedrooms, the living room, and the trim on the outside of the house. Pretty colours. Colours that looked good in the store but ugly on the walls. Fresh colours and stale colours. Bright colours and sad colours.

In big letters and small, all over the room— those words again:

What happens?

Duncan <u>slammed</u> the door.

All I can do these days is <u>slam</u> doors, he thought. That's all I can control.

His wife would *not* have the last word! He would walk to the hardware store and buy House for Sale signs. And he would hire someone to paint over all that mess in the basement. This was *his* house. This was *his* life, and *he* <u>was in charge!</u>

Duncan opened his front door. Fly King stood right on his <u>porch</u>, holding his skateboard.

"R. A. Dick," said the kid.

"What did you say to me?"

"R. A. Dick."

Duncan felt his hand <u>curl</u> into a <u>fist</u>.

"I've never hit a kid," Duncan said. "But if you or your <u>crowd</u> ever comes back here again, I will <u>beat</u> you <u>senseless</u>."

"Dude, I didn't say, 'You are a dick.' I said 'R. A. Dick.' You're awfully <u>touchy</u> for a rich old man with nothing to complain about."

"I'm not rich," Duncan said. The comment had caught him off-guard.

The kid looked at Duncan's house, then back to Duncan. "Dude," was all he said.

For some reason, that remark prompted Duncan to really look at the kid. His clothes looked like rags. Of course, ragged clothes could be the fashion, but still...

"Where are your parents?" Duncan asked.

"Oh, so now you're interested in other people?"

Fly King put his skateboard on the ground and got on it. "R. A. Dick," he said over his shoulder as he and his pack skated away.

Duncan locked the door behind him and headed out. He would get that House for Sale sign. And then he would track down this R. A. Dick.

If his wife had had an affair with this Dick guy, he, Duncan, would beat his brains out.

CHAPTER ELEVEN

Duncan found forty-seven Dicks in the phone book. None were R. A. Some were R. and some were A. He saw a Ronald and a Robert and a Rhonda, and an Albert and an Anita and an Abernathy.

Duncan decided to call them all.

Calling up strangers. Asking them if they had slept with his wife. This was not something he would usually do in the course of a day. But he was feeling more than a little crazy by this point. He did not care what people thought.

He sat with the phone by the front window, looking at the big bright House for Sale sign on the lawn. While he called people, he'd keep an eye out for anyone stopping to look at his house. He called right down the list of people named "Dick." Many hung up on him. One lady invited him to come over for supper. Two of the people had died, and one phone had been disconnected. He left seven messages on answering machines. Thinking of all the trouble he was causing made him laugh.

"I've gone around the bend," he said. And he took another drink.

But he was no closer to solving the problem.

And his son's car was pulling into the driveway.

Duncan thought of turning off the lights and pretending not to be home. But he was too late. His son was coming in the front door.

"Mom's library is gone," was the first thing Bobby said.

"It's the middle of the week," Duncan said. "Did you get the day off work?"

"She loved that library," Bobby said. "She wrote me letters about it. You're selling the house?"

Duncan walked past Bobby and went into the kitchen. His son, of course, would want lunch.

Several days' worth of dishes sat in the sink.

"Wow, Dad. Mom would never leave dirty dishes lying around."

"You should know," Duncan replied. "You dirtied enough of them. What are you doing here in the middle of the week?"

Bobby put some of the dishes on the counter so he could put the stopper into the sink drain. He added dish soap and turned on the tap.

Duncan turned the water off.

"Leave the damn dishes. I asked you a question."

Instead of replying, Bobby opened the fridge door.

"Where's all the food?" he asked. "Mom always kept lots of food."

"Yeah, well, your mother is dead," Duncan said. His words sounded mean even to him, but he was a little drunk and didn't care.

"You need someone to take care of things around here," Bobby said. "Run the house. Do the laundry."

"I've hired a cleaner," Duncan lied. He could see where this was leading. He knew without looking that Bobby's car was full of his stuff. He had quit his job or got himself fired and wanted to come back home.

"You don't want a stranger here."

Duncan leaned against the stove. "Let me guess, Bobby. Your boss didn't understand you."

"They just plain lied about the job! I thought it was going to be something special. They had me doing the dirty work. It was beneath me. I quit on principle. I have a master's degree!"

"I know," Duncan said. "I paid for it."

"Anyway, it's just as well. You are not managing here on your own."

Bobby took a take-out box of left-over chicken wings out of the fridge and sat down at the kitchen table.

Duncan plugged the kettle in and spooned instant coffee into a cup. For a while the kitchen was silent except for the sounds of Bobby eating and the kettle heating up.

When his coffee was made, Duncan sat at the table with his son.

"You gave up your apartment." It was a statement, not a question.

"The landlord was an idiot," Bobby said. "Says I owe him money. Really, he was charging way too much for that place. I had to make a statement. And that stuff he said I ruined. It was garbage when I moved in!"

"You're being sued." Again, it was a statement, not a question.

"How much are you selling the house for?" Bobby asked.

"What you really want to know is, are you going to get some of the money," Duncan said.

"She was my mother." Bobby pouted, his cheek stained with wing sauce. "I should have something to remember her by."

"Her glass animals are in the dining room," Duncan said. "Help yourself."

He took a drink of his coffee. It was hot and burned his throat. "You're young," Duncan said. "You're healthy. You are well-educated. You have nothing to tie you down. You could be living anywhere and doing anything. I don't understand you."

"You never took the time to understand me," Bobby told him. "You never once asked me what I wanted."

Duncan slammed his hand on the table.

"You cannot say that!" he said. "All I did was ask you what you wanted and then try to get it for you. You want to play hockey? I buy you all the gear, the best skates. You decide to quit after one game? No problem. You want to go on the expensive school trip? Then you back out when it's too late to get the money back? All right, anything, so long as you are happy. Boy, was your mother angry with me about that! You want that fancy bike? No problem. Leave it out in the rain so that it gets rusted after the first month? Of course you need another one. You want to live in the basement and play video games for three years after finally finishing university? Anything you want!"

"I stayed so long because Mom was lonely," Bobby said. "I stayed to keep her company."

"You stayed because you're lazy. Too lazy to get a job and too lazy to keep a job. I've told you that over and over."

"If I'm lazy, it's your fault . . ."

Duncan kept talking over him.

"You say you stayed to keep your mother company? Your mother didn't need company— not anyone's company, not yours and certainly not mine! Every spare minute, she had her head in some book. When she did bother to talk to me at all, she said she was tired of cleaning up after you. Twenty-eight years old and she was still trying to get you to do your own laundry. You were not company for her. You were a chore!"

By now they were both on their feet.

"All right. Maybe so," Bobby yelled. "I'm man enough to admit that I could have been a better son. But you were a lousy husband. Mom was lonely. You were never there for her."

"Your mother did not need me!" Duncan roared from deep within his gut. "She did not need me, and she did not need you! All she needed were those damn books. Why did she marry me? I could have married someone who wanted to be with me, not someone who shut me out all the time. Maybe I *was* a bad husband. But she did not need me! She just wanted me ... to go away ... so she could read."

Speaking such a deep truth made Duncan drop to his knees. He sobbed. He felt that he had spent his entire life alone. To his son, he was a wallet. To his wife, he was a noise.

He got himself under control and stood up.

"We're through here," he said to Bobby. "You can't move back in. I'm not giving you any money. You can have the rest of the chicken wings and your mother's glass animals if you want them.

But I don't want to see you again until you have straightened yourself out. Go. Live your life. And let me live mine."

Bobby stood in shocked silence for a moment. "I'll never forgive you for this," he said.

"I can live with that," Duncan told him. "Grow up, son. It's way past time."

Bobby moved slowly towards the door, as if he thought Duncan would call him back. Then he turned around and picked up the rest of the chicken wings. Duncan sat at the table with his coffee. He didn't look up when his son walked out the door, got in his car, and drove away.

But he had the strongest feeling that Tess was with him, sitting across the table, nodding and smiling.

CHAPTER TWELVE

Duncan couldn't sit at the kitchen table forever. After a while, he had to move to the sofa to watch TV.

He picked up the *TV Guide,* looking for something worth watching. He looked at the page listing all the movies, and he read the descriptions. A lot of the movies were about either blowing things up or kids becoming pop stars.

Duncan felt a sense of peace he hadn't felt since Tess's death. He was so sure she had been in the kitchen with him. He was so sure she was happy with him—in that moment, anyway. For once, she was not angry at him or just putting up with him. He smiled now as he thought about what he had said to Bobby. How she seemed to agree with him.

The two of them had done what they had to do about their greedy, freeloading son.

"We'll get it figured out, Tess," he said. "It's all going to be all right."

And then his eyes landed on something.

It was a movie listing: *The Ghost and Mrs. Muir*. Based on the novel by R. A. Dick.

That was all it said.

Duncan grabbed the remote and turned the television to the right channel. Humphrey Bogart and Lauren Bacall were kissing. Duncan recognized the movie: *To Have and Have Not*. He checked the *TV Guide* again. *The Ghost and Mrs. Muir* had been on the day before. He had missed it.

He threw the *TV Guide* on the sofa and called Kevin.

"R. A. Dick is the name of a writer," Duncan said. "Start checking. I'll be right there."

He went out to the garage. It was empty. His car was still being repaired. How would he get to the thrift store?

"Going somewhere, bro?" Fly King was at his elbow.

"Don't you have a home to go to?" Duncan asked him. "Don't your parents wonder where you are?"

Fly King lifted up an extra skateboard.

"It will get you there fast, man."

"Are you crazy? I'm not going to ride that thing. I'm nearly seventy years old. I'll fall off. I'll break a hip. I'll be killed in the streets."

The kid shrugged. "Maybe."

Duncan was about to call the kid an uncaring little jerk, but then he thought for a second. The walk to the thrift store would be long, and not pretty. The buses did not run very often and would not take him straight there anyway. And taxis took forever to get to his house.

"What do I do?" he asked Fly King.

"Just step on it," the kid said. "Step on it and let it roll."

So Duncan did just that.

He stepped on the skateboard.

And he let it roll.

"You never want to try something new," Tess would tell him. "You only want to do the things you have always done. You want to eat the same food, wear the same clothes, play the same game, and see the same people."

"Look at me now, Tess," he yelled as he zoomed down the street. "Look at me now!"

CHAPTER THIRTEEN

Kevin and Duncan almost didn't find the book.

They searched through the shelves, looking for any book written by R. A. Dick.

"R. A. Dick is a pen name," Kevin said. "The writer's real name was Josephine Aimee Campbell Leslie."

"No wonder she made it shorter," Duncan said.

"She was Irish," Kevin added. "She wrote three books. The most successful was *The Ghost and Mrs. Muir*. I looked it up online."

"Did you find out how the book ends?"

"No. But I found out that it was made into a movie and a television series."

"Never heard of it." Duncan shoved aside another pile of books. They were almost through the shelves. "What if you sold it already?"

"Then we will try the library, the bookstores, and the internet. There must be more than one copy in the world."

Duncan did not think he had the strength to go through all that. He started looking through the last shelf. He got to the end without finding any book by R. A. Dick.

And then he spotted the corner of something peeking out from under the bookshelf.

He knew it was the right book even before he reached down to pick it up.

He held it in his hands.

The Ghost and Mrs. Muir.

"What happens?" said his wife's voice inside his head.

"I found it," Duncan said to Kevin.

The book was small and thin, and its cover was black with white letters. On the front was a picture of an old sea captain in a dark blue cap.

"Yes, that's it," Kevin said. "You found it."

"I'm going to go home now and read it. And that will be the end of that. Tess will be happy, and I will be able to get on with my life."

"Good," said Kevin. "If that's what you want."

"Absolutely," Duncan said. "What do I owe you for this?"

Kevin waved his hand. "It's a gift. From one widower to another."

"Thanks." Duncan shook Kevin's hand. "Thanks for everything."

He made his way to the door, then turned back. He needed the answer to one question.

"When you found the insurance papers, what happened to your husband?"

"He disappeared," Kevin said.

"Did he ever come back?"

Kevin looked really sad. "Not yet."

Duncan nodded slowly, then left the shop.

He had a lot to think about.

CHAPTER FOURTEEN

Duncan went home and read.

He read the first line of the book to himself, and then he read it again out loud:

Mrs. Muir was a little woman.

The words made him think of his wife. As he spoke them, Tess appeared in the La-Z-Boy chair across the room. Mr. Snuffles, the cat, trotted over and sat by the chair. Duncan could hear him purring.

Duncan sat on the sofa with his feet on the coffee table and a cup of coffee at his side. He read out loud until the coffee got cold. Then he made a fresh cup and kept on reading.

Duncan could not remember the last time he had read a book. The teachers had made him read in school. Endless questions and essays and exams always followed. Reading was a chore. It was homework. It was something to get out of doing if he could. If he couldn't get out of reading, it was something to do quickly. Something to rush through, so he could do the things he liked to do.

He had never read a book because he wanted to.

In *The Ghost and Mrs. Muir*, Mrs. Muir's first name was Lucy. Her husband had died. Everyone around her thought they had the right to tell her what she should do. But she had her own ideas. She made her own life.

As he read, Duncan found himself cheering for her. He lost himself in the story until the room got dark. When he had to turn on a lamp, he was surprised to find himself in his own house. He had felt as if he were in Gull Cottage, Lucy's home by the sea.

"Is this what our life was like for you?" he asked the ghost of his wife. She just smiled.

He kept reading.

Duncan read as much as he could that day, until he started to nod off. He hated to stop reading, but he marked his place at page seventy-five. Then he went to bed, slept soundly, and got up early to go back to his reading.

While he was reading, he saw Tess, sitting and enjoying the story. But he knew from her face that she had already read this part. By late morning, he had only a few short chapters left. That's when he saw her sit up straight and even lean forward.

"This is what you have been waiting for, isn't it?" he asked her. "It is the ending you want to know about. Now you will find out what happens."

His wife smiled and nodded. He saw her ghost face sparkle in a way that he had rarely seen when she was alive.

He was afraid that if he finished the story, she would go. And he wanted her to stay.

"That's enough for today," he said, gently closing the book. "Come back tomorrow. Maybe we'll read some more."

Duncan watched her fade away. He was once more alone.

He looked down at the little book in his hand.

"She'll be back," he said to the cat. "She'll be back with us again."

CHAPTER FIFTEEN

The House for Sale sign came down.

The dining room furniture went back into the basement.

And the library went back into the dining room. But Duncan put up the bookshelves along the walls. That way, they didn't block off the living room, as they had before.

At first, Duncan put books on the shelves that he thought his wife would like. Then he decided to look for books *he* might like, too. He had enjoyed reading about the sea captain, so he looked for more sea stories. Reading them led him to novels about war, and they led to novels about other countries. Each book he read made him want to read something else.

The Ghost and Mrs. Muir stayed on the coffee table. Unfinished. There was plenty of time to finish it in the future. He wanted Tess to stick around for a while.

Duncan read his books aloud every day, and when he did, Tess appeared in her chair and listened.

Why didn't Tess just pick up *The Ghost and Mrs. Muir* and read the ending for herself? Duncan did not know. Maybe ghosts didn't work that way. Maybe she wanted them to finish the book together. He didn't mind not knowing why. He just liked having her back.

"We got a letter from Bobby," he said to Tess several months later. "He said he has a good new job. He's working really hard, and I have no right to call him 'lazy' ever again."

Tess never answered him, but he could tell what she was feeling. You can't live with someone for forty years and not know her moods. The news that their son had finally grown up made her very happy.

Duncan didn't see Tess every night. Sometimes he didn't feel like reading. He spent a lot of time down at the Good Shepherd Thrift Store, helping Kevin. One of his golf buddies asked him to help out with the kids at the community centre. Some evenings he was tired out from all his volunteer work. He sat in front of the television, watching the Golf Channel, just as he had in the old days.

Whenever he watched TV for too long, though, things would start happening. Pots and pans banged together in the kitchen. The cat jumped all over him, chasing an invisible mousie.

Then Duncan would reach for the remote. In one smooth move, he'd turn off the TV, pick up a book, and start to read.

And when he looked up from the sofa, he'd see his wife, his wonderful Tess. There she would sit, in the La-Z-Boy, being with him.

Good Reads Series

All Night by Alan Cumyn

The Stalker by Gail Anderson-Dargatz

Coyote's Song by Gail Anderson-Dargatz

Bed and Breakfast by Gail Anderson-Dargatz

The Break-In by Tish Cohen

Tribb's Troubles by Trevor Cole

In From the Cold by Deborah Ellis

The Clear-Out by Deborah Ellis

New Year's Eve by Marina Endicott

Home Invasion by Joy Fielding

The Day the Rebels Came to Town by Robert Hough

Picture This Anthony Hyde

Listen! by Frances Itani

Missing by Frances Itani

Shipwreck by Maureen Jennings

The Picture of Nobody by Rabindranath Maharaj

The Hangman by Louise Penny

Love You to Death by Elizabeth Ruth

Easy Money by Gail Vaz-Oxlade

About the Author

 Deborah Ellis is an award-winning author and a long-time peace activist. She has worked as a women's mental health counsellor and volunteered at refugee camps in Afghanistan. Deborah's bestselling series *The Breadwinner Trilogy* is based on a story told to her by a refugee. Deborah lives in Simcoe, Ontario.

Also by Deborah Ellis:

The Breadwinner
Parvana's Journey
A Company of Fools
Mud City
The Heaven Shop
Jackal in the Garden
I Am a Taxi
Jakeman
Sacred Leaf
No Safe Place
In From the Cold
No Ordinary Day
My Name is Parvana

Manufactured by Amazon.ca
Bolton, ON